Responding to Challenging Behaviour

Jo Pimlott

Assistant Director, Midlands Centre for Youth Ministry

Nigel Pimlott

Youth Work Development Advisor, Frontier Youth Trust

GROVE BOOKS LIMITED
RIDLEY HALL RD   CAMBRIDGE   CB3 9HU

Contents

The Cover Illustration is a photograph by Nigel Pimlott with thanks to Sarah, Jono and Matt

First Impression December 2005
ISSN 1748-3492
ISBN 1 85174 610 2

Introduction

1

The headline in the local paper read 'Yobs Reign of Terror!'

The story continued to describe a gang of teenagers running riot in the town, causing significant damage and hurling abuse at local people. It would be nice if this was an imagined story, inflated by a keen journalist looking for a sensational scoop, but sadly, it is not. We know it is true because we know the young people involved.

At the youth project we volunteer in, some of these young people have been very challenging. Pete ripped a radiator off the wall, Mandy set off the fire alarm, John tore a sign off the building, Col, Mickey and Chris have all stolen Playstation games, Emma and Liz were found self-harming, persons unknown send regular greetings to us via graffiti, Lee is enjoying the pleasure of Her Majesty's hospitality, volunteers and staff, Sarah, Claire and Mark have all had their cars vandalized, Sarah and Mark have also been assaulted, Nigel was called a bald ba****d (not quite true—he does have some hair left!) and some of these young people and others are currently 'helping the police with their enquiries' regarding a number of other incidents.

Having read this, you could easily form the impression that we are not very competent youth workers and you might recommend that we stop what we are doing. However, we have a well-trained and skilled team, one of the most highly regarded projects in the area and are working effectively with around two hundred young people each month. The difficulty is that numbers of these young people have issues and problems which manifest themselves in a range of challenging behaviours.

Many town and inner-city housing estates experience similar problems, as do some rural areas where there is little for young people to do

Our area has social challenges and problems associated with poverty and social exclusion. But many town and inner-city housing estates experience similar problems, as do some rural areas where there is little for young people to do. Even in areas which would be perceived as middle-class, the behaviour of a minority can pose a real challenge to those involved in youth work.

Many churches, organizations and Christian youth workers are increasingly seeking to reach out to young people in their communities. In doing so, they also inevitably engage with the pain, boredom, hurt, angst and frustration that some of these young people experience. The result is often conflict, stress and discouragement. Some churches pull the plug on community-based youth work and retreat to the safer confines of their worship services, Bible studies and Alpha courses. Some youth workers struggle with the pressure and find their own coping mechanisms through alcohol, caffeine, pills or time off with stress-related illness. Others simply stop doing youth work and either opt for a career change or never volunteer again. Others press on, seeing their work with young people as 'mission,' seeking to reach out to young people with God's love and compassion.

This booklet is aimed at all those who are seeking to engage with young people in a broad range of contexts. We recognize that this may include full and part-time youth workers, volunteers, ministers, those involved in uniformed organizations and numerous others. We will, however, use the terms 'youth workers' or 'workers' throughout for simplicity's sake. We have considered the title carefully and deliberately chosen the word 'responding' to sum up our intention. Expressions such as 'dealing with,' 'managing' and 'surviving' can present a very negative and controlling approach. By contrast, this booklet seeks to help youth workers empower those they work with to make their own informed choices as equal members of society, embracing both the privileges and responsibilities that such membership entails.

We will seek to define challenging behaviour, explore some of its causes and then consider three practical issues: establishing a positive context in which to work, responding on the spot to challenging behaviour and developing longer-term strategies to address deeper issues. Inevitably, the limitations of a short booklet mean that we cannot hope to tackle every issue in depth, nor can we take into account every context and situation. Finally, we will briefly consider some personal survival strategies for youth workers. All these considerations are set in the context of theological reflection, which might best be summarized by reflecting on Jesus' great commission (Matthew 28:18–20). When he commands that we make disciples of all 'people groups,' this inevitably includes young people and this missionary mandate should continue to inspire and challenge us to go out and make a difference in our communities. Richard Passmore helpfully encapsulates this challenge:

> We need to meet these young people where they are. We need to love them unconditionally in the scandalous way Jesus did, care with relentless tenderness and get involved in the mess of the world around them.[1]

What is Challenging Behaviour? 2

A recent article in *The Times* referred to the 'ASBO generation'—a very different description from the more commonly used 'Generation Y,' 'mosaics,' and 'millennials.' It is interesting to see how the Anti-Social Behaviour Order—a key law and order response to challenging behaviour—appears almost to define this generation. At the time of writing, a debate is raging about whether 'hoodies' and baseball caps should be banned from shopping centres. A survey by the magazine *Young People Now* found that 71% of press articles concerning young people had a negative tone, only 14% were positive and 48% of articles about crime and violence depicted a young person as the perpetrator[2]. The impression that every young person in the country is out to attack, mug or vandalize property is far from the truth. Most young people grow up without committing crime or engaging in anti-social behaviour[3].

Whilst not wishing to underestimate the effect that some individuals' behaviour can have on communities, groups and individuals within them, we must avoid stereotyping or 'demonizing' young people or being prejudiced against them. Closer investigation reveals that young people are responsible for only a relatively low percentage of crime in the UK and are equally likely to find themselves victims of it.

Challenging behaviour covers a whole range of issues that affect young people. The table below illustrates the percentage of young people that might be involved in a variety of situations, behaviours and circumstances that present challenges to not only churches and Christian youth workers, but to society as a whole.

% of Young People	Characteristic
Less than 1%	Are permanently excluded from school
	Are imprisoned
	Had teenage pregnancy
	Are on child protection register
	Are looked after now (in care)

1-5%	Are, or have been, looked after
	Persistently truant or offend
	Have tried hard drugs before age of 18
5-10%	Have no qualifications at 16
	Abuse solvents
	Are not in education, employment or training (NEET)
	Criminally offend (up to 3 offences)
10-30%	Run away from home
	Have mental health problems
	Have committed a criminal offence in the last year
	Truant occasionally
	Are NEET at some point between ages 16-18

Source: Nottingham County Council 2005

Some of these circumstances and characteristics will present themselves to youth workers, whilst others may be more apparent to others who work with young people, like teachers, health professionals and personal advisors. For youth workers the list below perhaps covers some of the issues, which manifest and cause challenges in a group or community situation:

Self harm	Bullying
Drug and alcohol abuse	Boredom
Harassment of individuals	Begging
Prostitution	Creating noise and disturbance
Vandalism or graffiti	Withdrawn behaviour
Joy riding	Anger
Conflict	Spitting
Attention seeking	Swearing

Racism, sexism	Disruptiveness
Abuse of equipment	Misuse of the internet
Smoking	Winding up volunteers and staff
Belonging to a large group or gang	Flirting with volunteers and staff
Throwing things	Verbal abuse
Wandering about during sessions	Poor concentration

This list is by no means exhaustive and it must be emphasized that different youth workers will have more or less tolerance for particular aspects of behaviour. For some, an individual not concentrating during a Bible study session can be very frustrating, whilst for others responding to teenage prostitution might be the challenge. Some workers will be irritated by people talking or texting whilst something else is taking place, whilst for others the 'cut off' point might be physical assault of staff. Different environments call for different responses, and it is not our intention to be prescriptive about what should and should not be allowed in a given situation, but rather to provide some frameworks to enable workers to respond more aptly to the challenges that they face.

Whatever the challenge, we need to bear in mind that the context into which we are working is the cutting edge of mission. Engaging with young people in our communities can be hard work. It needs careful planning and consideration and adequate support and resources to sustain and develop it. Youth workers often find themselves wrestling with the seemingly conflicting aims of seeking to model God's love and acceptance to those they are working with, whilst also seeking to set clear and appropriate boundaries and create safe environments for young people. We see clearly in Scripture how God's love for humanity is expressed through the setting of clear boundaries for their protection and well-being (Genesis 2:16–17). Similarly in his work with the early churches, we are given a glimpse, through his letters, of the boundaries Paul sets in place to enable these emerging congregations to work together effectively (see for example 1 Corinthians 14:29–31, Ephesians 5:25–32, 1 Thessalonians 3:12–22). From a practical point of view, an understanding of the causes of challenging behaviour can help youth workers with some of the tensions this raises.

3

The Causes of
Challenging Behaviour

Much of what we hear in the press and from politicians appears to focus on the outcomes of anti-social behaviour.

This is perhaps inevitable, as it reflects the concerns of society as a whole, sells newspapers and potentially attracts votes. Less prominent in the public domain is the conversation about addressing the underlying causes of challenging behaviour.

Sometimes it appears that there is a competition between the political parties as to who can be the toughest and most draconian in their approaches to tackling these challenges—a process that most research undertaken on the subject concludes does not work![4] In most cases where young people exhibit challenging behaviour, the issue presented is generally not the real issue at all. Youth workers need to be aware of the underlying issues, problems and needs which often are the root causes of disruption, attention-seeking or aggressive behaviour. The real roots of these types of challenging behaviours are how young people come to terms with some of the big issues in life. Research suggests that young people have a much higher risk of offending if they have:

- A troubled home life, including poor parenting, criminal family members, violence or abuse
- Peer group pressure
- Poor attainment at school, truancy and school exclusion
- Deprivation such as poor housing or homelessness[5]

It must be acknowledged that political efforts have been made in recent years to address some of these issues. There has been a greater focus on tackling child poverty, increasing parental skills, reducing truanting and substance abuse and developing higher achievement at school. Whilst these approaches are to be welcomed by the Christian community and are consistent with a holistic view of the gospel, they often still do not go to the roots of the problems and challenges. Our own observations would suggest that the following also appear to be consistent factors in 'undoing' a young person's perspective on life, and consequently affecting their behaviour:

- Coping with loss
- Having low self esteem
- Dealing with false expectations
- Lacking a sense of love and belonging
- Struggling with their sexual identity
- Receiving repeated criticism

If we also consider the spiritual dimension of these issues, we see in many cases considerable woundedness and fragmentation in the lives of many young people.

Long term, relational youth work can provide the opportunity for issues such as these to be addressed on a strategic basis, particularly where workers are seeking to network strongly with other agencies and individuals involved. In other cases, youth workers may simply be performing a 'holding' or 'bridging' type role, finding ways of helping the young person within the context of their relationship and resources. If, as Bosch suggests, 'God's yes to the world reveals itself, to a large extent, in the church's missionary engagement in respect of the realities of injustice, oppression, poverty, discrimination, and violence'[6] then ongoing involvement with young people demonstrating challenging behaviour reflects the very heart and mission of God in relation to the communities around us.

In addition to the issues above it is also worth mentioning some other potential causes of challenging behaviour:

- Learning difficulties, autistic spectrum disorders and conditions such as attention deficit disorder and attention hyperactivity deficit disorder can result in behaviour that might challenge groups and workers. The scope of this booklet does not allow an in-depth exploration of these issues, but workers can find specialist help and support through national organizations and networks.

- Development factors must not be underestimated when it comes to young people's challenging behaviour. Challenging behaviour can simply be a manifestation of physical, socio-emotional, intellectual and spiritual development and it is helpful for workers to grow their understanding of some of the implications of this.

- Group dynamics can also play a significant part. The mix of ages, gender mix and maturity levels within can all conspire to produce very challenging youth work. Group dynamics might need to be changed to address problems here, with the use of single sex groups or different age range approaches. Similarly the stage of development of the group may be a significant factor. 'Storming' and the testing of boundaries is a normal part of group development and workers may need to develop their group-work skills to facilitate these processes. Groups which have been through this are often far more effective and productive in the long term.

- Cultural issues can also be a factor, particularly subcultural clashes between groups of young people.

- Levels of expectation from both workers and young people can be a key issue. This will be addressed later.

- Past experience and group culture can also be a factor. Once a club or group gets a reputation for problems, it can be very hard to shake this off. A culture can be created where young people come expecting to behave badly. In one local monthly disco we ran for teenagers, young people used to save up their grievances and fights for that particular night and the results were very stressful for the team involved. Sometimes a group or project needs re-inventing or changing significantly, so that a new culture can be established.

- The general tendency for young people to test and push boundaries until they feel secure must also be borne in mind.

In order to take these issues seriously, a three-stage strategy can be seen as a way of responding to issues of challenging behaviour. The first stage, culture-setting, is more preventative in approach and addresses areas of policy, procedures and expectations. The second stage explores the challenge of responding to the immediate crisis when problems arise and the third seeks to unpack the 'why' of the problem or situation.

> Whilst visiting some youth workers in Birmingham I got chatting to a young person who seemed to be the gang leader of a group of older Asian boys. He was a very likeable and amenable boy who clearly had the gift of the gab. He was very confident and astute. We talked about what he got up to and some of the issues about local young people in the community. He then said that, 'we [the gang] used to cause lots of trouble in the area, but we have settled down now.' I wondered what might have caused this change of heart and settling down. Sadly, we won't ever know as the conversation moved on and then drew to a close. It reminded me that the vast majority of young people do 'settle down' and grow up to be integrated members of the community.
>
> *Nigel Pimlott*

Culture Setting

4

> Therefore everyone who hears these words of mine and puts them into practice is like a wise man who built his house on the rock. The rain came down, the streams rose, and the winds blew and beat against that house; yet it did not fall, because it had its foundation on the rock.
>
> Matthew 7:24–25

If youth workers are to respond effectively to challenging behaviour, they need to be well prepared. Jesus, in his well-known parable about the wise and foolish builders, emphasizes the importance of good foundations and culture-setting is really about making sure the right foundations for the work are in place. Metaphorical storms cannot be avoided in youth work, but the quality of what has been built will be significantly higher if the work is effectively underpinned. Workers may need to 'react' when situations arise, but significant stress can be avoided by proactive planning beforehand. Although it is impossible to prepare for every eventuality, setting procedures and protocols in place will help all those involved be clear about what is expected, how they should respond in a situation and may even help prevent some issues arising.

Policies and Procedures

This anticipation of events and subsequent intervening action is one of the keys to responding well to challenging behaviour. Appropriate policies provide a firm foundation for safe and effective work with young people and are essential if we are to be respected by those in the wider community. A sense of excellence in our approach to the professional aspects of the work will glorify God and help us establish and develop 'a good reputation with outsiders.' Where workers have a clear understanding of these policies, there is less potential for misunderstanding, lack of clarity in ground rules and 'splitting'—young people playing one worker off against the other.

As a minimum requirement, those working with young people should have child protection and health and safety policies in place and undertake risk assessment on facilities and activities. In addition to this it may be helpful to develop a behaviour policy, which focuses specifically on what behaviour is expected within the group or club and what the potential sanctions are if rules are broken. Involving the young people in the development of such a policy is a positive way of raising and discussing behaviour issues. Rules regarding behaviour need to be clear and well-reasoned and in this case, less really is more. In one club we work in, for example, the only rule about swearing is that bad language should not be used as a weapon against others. Rules have been kept to a minimum, but the rules that do exist have been negotiated and agreed with the young people and are maintained very firmly. Once ground rules have been agreed, they should be clearly communicated. Word of mouth and eye-catching posters or notices in the venue are helpful here. Workers should not be apologetic about communicating or enforcing ground rules, as they exist as much for the benefit of the young people as the workers.

It is important to have an agreed policy on reporting incidents. The normal process would be for a worker to fill in an incident report form, following any occasion where young people have behaved in an inappropriate manner, particularly where any damage to property or physical injury has been caused. This information is important as it may be needed if questions are asked as to how the incident was handled, if criminal charges are brought or if a young person has been restrained and later makes an accusation against a worker. Decisions need to be taken about where such recordings are kept and what is done with them following an incident.

Once relevant policies and procedures are in place, it is essential to ensure that all workers receive adequate training to equip them for their responsibilities and that appropriate induction, support and supervision processes are established.

> We lately had trouble with one girl in our youth group. She was rude, crude and would beat someone up each week. She makes the youth group an unsafe place for everyone else. I really struggled with what to do for several weeks then eventually arranged to meet her and told her her behaviour was totally inappropriate and that as a result she was banned indefinitely from one of the two youth groups she came to and was on probation at the other one. We agreed conditions. The outcome has been very positive and she is starting to integrate once again. On reflection, the important thing was to take very decisive action; less important was doing exactly the right thing. I was only able to take such decisive action because we had very clearly set out boundaries. *Gary Brown*

Sanctions

The consequences of disruptive or aggressive behaviour need to be agreed and communicated in advance of any situations occurring. This enables workers to intervene with confidence and maintain consistency, as well as depersonalizing interventions. Where possible it is advisable to make sanctions as appropriate to the behaviour as possible. For example, where something has been stolen or damaged, the most appropriate sanction will include some form of reparation. Where possible, sanctions should reflect the values of the church or organization. A good example of this is restorative justice, where all those involved in a particular conflict or incident are drawn together to agree how to deal with the repercussions of what has happened. In this approach the person who has done wrong is given the opportunity to understand and acknowledge the impact of the action on others, and sanctions are sought which are appropriate to the context. Meeting face to face with those who have been hurt or affected by their behaviour has proved effective in many cases in addressing young people's behaviour on a longer term basis and reflects a holistic and redemptive approach, which is particularly appropriate in a Christian context.[7]

Sanctions may include being asked to leave a session or a ban from future sessions. The issue of banning young people from sessions or groups is often a difficult one. Some youth workers feel that banning undermines values of acceptance and unconditional love, communicating rejection to those often already rejected. It can result in young people hanging around outside buildings and some young people simply refuse to leave or seek to re-enter the building. However, experience would suggest that for some individuals, being banned from a session or group is sometimes the only option and it sends a very clear message that certain behaviours are not acceptable. It demonstrates that workers take issues seriously and offers an opportunity for the worker to re-negotiate boundaries with the young person concerned before they return to the group.

The issue of contacting parents or carers can be a difficult one, and while it is not always possible or advisable to get parental support in situations where young people are behaving badly, building relationships with families can be helpful in seeking a holistic approach to ongoing difficulties. It can also be enlightening for many reasons. Sometimes youth workers make assumptions about families based on a young person's behaviour, which turn out to be completely misguided. Visiting families and building purposeful relationships with them can be a valuable part of a youth worker's role in a community.

One of the important decisions to make when considering sanctions is to agree whether and when police help will be called and a policy on pressing charges for criminal behaviour. Agreeing this in advance of situations arising depersonalizes any future actions or prosecutions.

As well as considering the issue of sanctions it is important to find ways of rewarding positive behaviour. Starting a volunteer scheme or youth forum, for example, can increase young people's sense of ownership and participation in a project.

> We've found that rewarding positive behaviour is a really good way to respond to challenging behaviour. For example we've just introduced

a 'gold star trip' scheme, where we go on a trip every 6–8 weeks that young people can only be part of by invitation. Everyone starts off with 5 gold stars, which are lost when a young person receives a warning. The people with the most gold stars left just before the trip get an invitation. We were worried at fist it might be a bit 'school-ish,' but its working really well—we have seen a radical change in behaviour in the last couple of months. *Zoe Bell*

Planning Issues

When a church asks for advice on youth work, we are increasingly beginning with the same question: 'What is it you are trying to do?' Having a sense of calling to the work is vitally important in terms of sustaining momentum and enthusiasm. If the aim of the youth work is to reach young people with the gospel, then in mission terms, it must be on their patch and on their terms and understanding. Mission has always ultimately failed when a system of control is imposed upon a group.

We have come across several groups who set out on the journey of working with young people in their communities, only to abandon the work when things got difficult. They set out with a desire to bring young people into church but as they struggled to respond to challenging behaviours, the barriers went up and rather than being 'drawn in,' young people were increasingly 'thrown out.' Often, unrealistic expectations are the underlying problem here. It is worth noting again that increasingly the pattern and journey of discipleship for many young people with no previous church background is one of belong, believe, behave rather than the old paradigm of behave, believe, belong.

Establishing clear aims and objectives for any club is of primary importance in establishing values and culture. It may seem obvious, but it is important for workers to explore why young people come along and what they want from the group or club. Genuine dialogue of this kind should develop and increase a sense of ownership and belonging. It will also enable youth workers to provide relevant activities and increasingly involve young people in the delivery of provision. We have heard youth workers complaining about the behaviour of the young people, only to discover that activities were simply not relevant to those attending. If young people are coming along to meet with and chat to their friends and are then expected to sit in silence, they are unlikely to respond positively. If the key aim for a particular season of the youth work is to build strong relationships, for example, this might be better achieved through detached youth work, meeting young people on their territory, rather than doing a group in a church hall where youth workers have to enforce a lot of rules.

As well as overall aims, clear objectives should be set for each club, group and session. It is good practice to review these regularly and to evaluate how they are being met. A ten-minute team evaluation at the end of a session can be extremely helpful in evaluating objectives, identifying any problems or patterns of behaviour, supporting workers and increasing team cohesion.

Youth work is about informal education processes, in other words about learning and development, not about social control. Although specific behaviours will need to be challenged, broader behaviour issues should be addressed within the context of an educational process where young people are enabled to learn about respect, responsibility and treating others in ways that they would want to be treated. Where learning is taking place, activities should be relevant to the group and take into account different styles of learning. Some young people become disruptive simply because the worker is using a one-dimensional approach which is not suited to the young people. For example, a very active, high-energy group will get quickly bored doing work sheets!

> Being in a city centre church with its diverse population means I always have to be open to adapting material and changing the programme. I've found it's always useful to have a bank of games and activities to draw on at any time. Because I work in a team, it's been useful to have creativity sessions where we just pool our ideas. Then I can produce a resource that anyone who's leading can dip in and out of as needed.
>
> *Hannah Leigh*

Team Culture

Building a strong team—whether a team of two or ten—is a key advantage in addressing difficult issues. In some teams there can appear to be a jostling competitive atmosphere, where a key issue is a popularity contest around which worker the young people like most. It is vital to build a culture of co-operation rather than competition, where each team member is valued and people are encouraged to play to their strengths. A team member with a short temper may not be the best person to stay calm in a dispute where patience and level-headedness are needed. Similarly, certain team members will be skilled at listening, negotiation, building relationships, intervening firmly and so on. 1 Corinthians 12:14–26 paints a helpful picture of the way in which the members of Christ's body should need, value, honour and protect each other and grasping these truths will increase team effectiveness significantly. Within volunteer teams we can helpfully include people with all kinds of different gifts and skills to engage effectively with young people. Some will have a real sense of calling to reach out to and develop relationships with young people. Others may simply be willing to serve the vision, but can be encouraged to use their own skills and gifts to add to the quality of the work being undertaken.

Environment

Many groups debate the best environments to engage with young people. Whether the choice is the church hall, a local community centre, out in the streets through detached work or in a school, different environments are likely to produce different behaviour from the young people. Changing environments can be one way of addressing behaviour issues, either through moving venue or by creating a different 'feel' to the venue through the use of décor, posters, furniture, lighting, layout and the like. A sense of ownership can be engendered here by involving young people in decisions and processes of design and decoration. Many visitors to the centre we work in are surprised by the lack of vandalism to the youth drop in interior, but we put this down to the fact that young people were involved in choosing colours, furniture layout and the painting and decoration of the venue.

Spiritual Factors

It is worth mentioning that sometimes things go wrong because the enemy seeks to disrupt and cause problems. It is beyond the scope of this booklet to explore this fully, but the spiritual aspects of problems, whether reflected in an individual, group or project, cannot be underestimated. A prayerful approach to every aspect of the work is essential. We have seen significant changes in behaviour occur through targeted prayer and it may be worth seeking to recruit specific prayer backing for groups or individuals where there are consistent ongoing problems. Most churches have numerous people within them who would not engage with face-to-face youth work, but are happy to pray regularly if given the appropriate information and feedback. A prayerful approach helps us to maintain a godly attitude to those who may be causing us significant stress in a particular context. It is important to remember that we are not primarily struggling against 'flesh and blood' (Ephesians 6:12) but seeking to see the kingdom of God advance in our area. Whatever our theology on spiritual warfare, time spent considering a prayer strategy for the work will not be wasted.

> We ran an open youth club called 'The Yard' at our church in the middle of a council estate. Early sessions were hard work and far more about policing than building relationships. We hit on the idea of having prayer cover for the session but decided to have it on the premises so every night we met there were one or two people praying in the vestry—it meant that one of us could pop in with urgent requests and that for the younger leaders they could see us modelling prayer at the centre of our youth work and mission. *Paul and Sally Nash*

On the Spot Responses to Challenging Behaviour

5

> A huge storm came up. Waves poured into the boat, threatening to sink it. And Jesus was in the stern, head on a pillow, sleeping! They roused him saying, 'Teacher, is it nothing to you that we're going down?' Awake now, he told the wind to pipe down and said to the sea, 'Quiet! Settle down!' The wind ran out of breath; the sea became as smooth as glass. Jesus reprimanded the disciples: 'Why are you such cowards? Don't you have any faith at all?' (Mark 4:37–40 The Message)

Jesus' response to the storm illustrates quite helpfully the level-headedness required in responding to manifestations of challenging behaviour. Although inside we may be feeling a whirlwind of emotions, it is vitally important that we do not imitate the disciples and run around in panic fearing the worst, but that we respond calmly and appropriately. In many situations where challenging behaviour presents, youth workers have no time to consider the longer term and deeper issues involved and must simply provide a fast response 'holding role' to:

- Alleviate the immediate problem
- Ensure safety of the young person, other young people and workers
- Protect the physical environment
- Adhere to agreed policies and procedures

On-the-spot responses to challenging behaviour are by nature reactive. Workers will sometimes not have time to consider options but will need to intervene quickly. This underlines the importance of having thought through issues beforehand, being clear about responsibilities and having a firm grasp of policies and procedures. Although it is impossible to cover all eventualities, the following suggestions incorporate principles which will hopefully inform many situations and behaviours.

Levels of Awareness

In a club, drop in or other group situation, at least one worker should have an overview of what is happening in the room and keep an eye out for problems that might arise. Some situations can appear to blow up out of nowhere but often there are warning signs and workers should be aware of some of these.

This can be helped by:

- Maintaining a visible presence in the venue;
- Ensuring an adequate ratio of workers to young people and making sure workers are not left isolated in particular parts of a building;
- Allowing at least one worker to take a 'floating' role and keep an overview, without having to be absorbed in discussions or activities;
- Keeping an eye on 'hot spots'—toilets, for example, can often be key places for gossip, stirring and ally-building;
- Encouraging all workers to be aware of what is happening beyond their immediate conversation or activity.

Avoiding escalation

This is a key area to prevent situations from getting out of hand. It is not always easy to intervene early, but where workers see problems arising they should:

- Maintain a presence, listening and observing within view of the individuals involved;
- Try to isolate the individual or group that is causing the problem—an audience will make things worse;
- Avoid jumping to conclusions or making assumptions, seeking rather to find out what is going on or what has happened by carefully listening to all parties involved;
- Try not to get drawn into an argument or competition;
- Speak calmly, assertively and respectfully, seeking to manage their own responses to the situation and not to overreact. The voice should be kept low and slow and measured;
- Not push or 'interrogate' and remain aware of their non-verbal communication, avoiding defensive or aggressive body language. For example, holding the hands loosely at the side is non-aggressive;
- Avoid touching the other person as this can be perceived as aggressive, even if the gesture is only meant for comfort or reassurance;
- Try to explain what they see happening and, depending on the situation, suggest alternative courses of action to find 'win/win' solutions;
- Continually seek to calm the situation and bring about some sort of resolution.

Sometimes allowing a bit of 'time out' can calm the situation, for the worker as well as the young people involved. Be aware of personality clashes. Where a young person clashes with a particular worker this can increase tension. In such situations it may be preferable for others to intervene.

Negotiation

Negotiation is a skill that can be developed with practice and can be an invaluable tool in seeking to resolve conflict and respond to challenging behaviour. It is important, first of all, to be mindful of issues which are not negotiable. Where group or organizational policies need to be adhered to, for instance, or where a criminal offence has occurred, the situation will need to be approached assertively. In 'greyer' situations negotiation may enable a solution, resolution or way forward to be found. Some helpful things to bear in mind with regard to negotiation:

> *It is important, first of all, to be mindful of issues which are not negotiable*

- Seeking to understand what the individual or individuals are saying by employing active listening skills will demonstrate to them that they are being heard and enable workers to move forward with the appropriate information. Reflecting back what the person is saying, using their words, or reframing their words to demonstrate understanding are both helpful skills here.

- Seeking to depersonalize the problem or issue is vital in negotiation, for example, focusing on specific behaviour rather than personality or concentrating on the issue at hand rather than raking up any past history.

- Encouraging creative thinking can help in seeking to find ways forward. Trying to think of as many different solutions as possible and encouraging the young people involved to think of ideas can help generate some options. Offering a number of options can prevent individuals feeling trapped and encourage choice and responsibility. Finding ways of allowing people to save face can also be very important in conflict situations.

- Agreeing details is an important part of concluding a process of negotiation. This might involve pinning individuals down to a specific course of action, reviewing and summarizing what has been agreed and, if necessary, developing a contract outlining what is expected.

Sometimes, if discussions have become very heated and the individuals concerned are angry or upset, it may be necessary to negotiate discussing the issue at a later time when everyone has calmed down. However, a time should be arranged at that point so that the problem is not simply left 'hanging.' Similarly, if a young person storms off, it is important to take the next available opportunity to discuss the matter levelly and calmly.

Responding to Aggressive Behaviour

Many of the suggestions above are relevant to the issue of aggressive behaviour. It is important to develop an awareness of the particular culture of the young people involved in a group or club and to be aware that some behaviour is more cultural than genuinely aggressive. Clear boundaries and expectations are key here, but the following principles are important to underline:

- Seeking to anticipate aggression and diffuse situations can be effective prevention. This can be helped by looking for warning signs and not letting arguments escalate;
- Keeping calm is essential, no matter how individuals or groups react. However tempting it is to face aggression with aggression, workers should remain calm and assertive in their approach. Experience also suggests that a macho approach from male workers is not the best way of handling problems;
- The safety of the young people and workers should be the primary consideration. Where possible, aggression should be isolated and any audience drawn away from the area;
- It is important not to corner people and to give ways out which allow young people to save face.

I was running a holiday play scheme, when one day in the park a teenage lad with a history of aggressive and violent behaviour was running around brandishing a very large stick, hitting people and intimidating the younger children's group. I chased him around, asking him to give me the stick which he refused. Eventually I realized he was shouting 'get your own bloody stick!' and that he was misinterpreting my intentions rather drastically. So I stopped pursuing him, and explained that I didn't want a big stick to hit anyone with, rather that I didn't want him to have a stick around younger children. He was able to hear what I was saying and although reluctant for anyone else to end up with the stick, found the solution of mashing it up so that it could not longer be used as a weapon.   *Sam Richards*

Restraint

The issue of restraint is a grey area legally, and should be part of your Child Protection Policy. Sometimes youth workers face situations where young people put themselves or others at risk and immediate physical intervention is needed. However, responses must not overstep the mark. The Churches Child Protection Advisory Service advises that in such situations workers should:

- Request that the behaviour stops
- Speak with the young person to find out the cause of the upset
- Warn them that they will be asked to leave if the behaviour continues
- Warn them that continued disruptive behaviour might result in longer-term exclusion from the activity.

If someone is harming himself or herself or another person or property, other young people should be escorted to vacate the area where the disruption is occurring. At the same time, and with a second worker present, the individual should again be asked to stop. If this request is ignored workers may need to warn that they might have to call for additional help, for example, the police. In exceptional circumstances, and with the help of another, whilst police help is awaited, a worker might need to prevent young people from harming themselves, or others. In all circumstances, workers present should make appropriate recordings of the incident.[8]

We need to be realistic and observe that things do not always work out in a nice neat way. Sometimes, a young person will not leave the club, they will not stop throwing things at the windows or they continue verbally abusing others present. A decision will have to be made as to what action to take in these instances, bearing in mind the above principles.

> I was running a small group in a small basement room with only one exit up a spiral staircase to the door. One teenage lad with a history of poor self-control and aggressive behaviour lost his temper and started punching other group members. It was a rather confined space, and I decided to restrain and remove him for everyone's safety. I stood behind him and put my arms around him, restricting his arm movements, and then just lifted him off his feet and carried him up the stairs. I am a small woman, and it occurred to me halfway up the stairs that if he resisted I would not be able to carry him—but I don't think that occurred to him! In fact, I would describe this action as mirroring the way a parent would step in and provide external control to a toddler who has not got the self-control not to hurt themselves or others, and it successfully enabled him to cool off away from the situation that had angered him.
>
> *Sam Richards*

It is important to remember that conflict and confrontation can be stressful and distressing for the young people and workers involved. Youth workers should ensure that they seek appropriate support following an incident. Support may be part of a session review process, but may need additional time allocated.

Low Key Interventions

Much of the material above relates to more extreme cases of challenging behaviour, but in many cases low-key behaviour can be very disruptive and frustrating. Constant bickering, low-grade bullying or name-calling, attention-seeking and general silliness can disrupt groups and significantly affect the atmosphere and productivity of youth work. In many cases these are ongoing issues, which will need to be considered as part of a longer term response (see the next chapter) but there are practical things that can be done.

- Establishing, agreeing and maintaining ground rules within a group creates clear expectations. Agreement also needs to be reached as to who will maintain these ground rules—workers or the young people themselves.
- Highlighting and affirming appropriate individual contributions will underline expectations and reinforce positive behaviour. It is also helpful to refuse to condone inappropriate behaviour with laughter or attention.
- With dominant individuals, clear, assertive statements like 'I would like to hear what others have to say about this' should be used rather than put-downs, digs or ignoring.
- Helpful processes to prevent individuals dominating a group include working in pairs or sub-groups and feeding back, writing or drawing contributions on large pieces of paper or using a 'pretend microphone' or similar which is passed around when people wish to talk.
- Encouraging appropriate humour and creating space and time for young people to chat, have fun and catch up with each other is important in creating a warm, fun atmosphere.
- Where an individual or sub-group is disruptive, it may be helpful to have an adult move to sit with them to help focus attention or challenge behaviour quietly in a way that does not distract the whole group.

We used to have a girl who came to youth group who had severe learning difficulties. She found it difficult to be part of the group and would often insult other young people. What I found helpful was having a structure to our time together so that everyone had a time to speak. If people began speaking over one another, we could draw on the structure to ensure that everyone knew they would have an opportunity. Also beginning the session by having a look at the rules that had been created by the group and a discussion about them, laid out the guidelines right at the beginning.

Hannah Leigh

Longer Term Responses to Challenging Behaviour

6

A sustained, relational, long-term approach to working with a young person to address underlying causes of challenging behaviour requires a proactive youth worker and a willingness from the young person to begin the journey. These journeys might at times be painful, time-consuming and emotionally and spiritually draining. They can present some very real challenges for churches and Christian groups, which are often operated on a voluntary basis.

Many volunteers have other jobs, roles and responsibilities and the demand of having to follow through a piece of work with a young person can bring significant pressure to bear. However, there are immense rewards in seeing young people develop increased confidence, self esteem and responsibility, and these longer term approaches will often produce fruit quickly in terms of the immediate behaviour challenges presented in a group context. It is worth looking broadly across the church or organization to identify people with particular skills in this area. Sometimes, in a church context, there are people who would not be willing to run a youth group, but would be very happy mentor a young person on a one-to-one basis and would do this very effectively with the right training and support.

Intervention Plans

A helpful way to begin such a process is to develop an intervention plan for the individual situation. This will include identifying:

- The aims and objectives in working with the individual. 'Smart' (specific, measurable, achievable, realistic and time-bounded) objectives will really focus thinking and planning;
- The methods that will be most appropriate. These might include mentoring, one-to-one discipleship, encouraging a young person to get involved in a particular activity or group, involving other individuals or specialist organizations;
- How the work will be evaluated. This might include observation (for example of particular changes in behaviour), discussion with the young person, achievement of the objectives.

It is important in developing an intervention plan to discuss and explore this with the young person. They may not want to spend time one-to-one with a youth worker—they may have their own ideas about the kinds of help and support they need. A key part of valuing them and helping them own any process will be their involvement and ownership at the thinking and planning stage. It is also important for youth workers to be realistic about their own time availability, resources and expertise and not to make unrealistic promises that they will not be able to keep, which might only increase a young person's sense of rejection or disillusionment.

Networking and Referrals

Some churches and Christian groups seem very bad at asking for help. This may be tied up with the belief that the gospel should be all-sufficient and that if we cannot handle things on our own then it reflects badly upon our message. The good news is that Jesus seemed to have little hesitation in asking for help on numerous occasions. He involved the disciples in feeding the five thousand (Matthew 14:16–19), asked the woman at the well to give him a drink of water (John 4:7), invited himself to Zacchaeus's house (Luke 19:5) and sent two disciples to fetch a donkey for his ride into Jerusalem (Matthew 21:2).

The concept of joined up working has gathered momentum in recent times. Too many mistakes have been made by individual organizations trying to handle things on their own. Sadly, some high profile cases, like the Victoria Climbie case, have found churches at the forefront of bad practice in this regard. The types of young people who evidence severe traits of challenging behaviour need a lot of support and input. Often other organizations and service-providers are already involved with them and youth workers need to ensure that they are complementing rather than undermining this work.

A broad range of issues—addiction, self harm, depression, eating disorders—will often be more appropriately and effectively addressed by specialists. Careful involvement of young people in the processes of negotiating and finding specialist help is important here. It is not simply a case of passing the young person on to another organization. Workers may help the process by exploring the kinds of help young people want or need, providing information such as contact details or telephone numbers or accompanying them to an appointment or clinic. Workers need to follow their own child protection and confidentiality policies in relation to these kinds of referrals.

It is clear here that a network of contacts and sources of help and/or information is a key resource for workers seeking to engage long-term in responding to challenging behaviour. These contacts and sources can be broadly divided into two categories. Local networks might include schools, police, Local Authority youth service, drugs information, counselling services and other service providers. These can be drawn on for advice or information or may provide specialist help for a young person. It is helpful, where possible, for workers to seek to build effective, ongoing relationships here, which will not only be of benefit to the two organizations involved, but will also benefit the young people they serve. The second category comprises wider sources of help and information, which may be national or regional and may include help lines, web sites, specialist organizations and service providers.

Personal Survival Strategies 7

> Elijah was afraid and ran for his life...He came to a broom tree, sat under it and prayed that he might die. 'I have had enough, Lord,' he said. 'Take my life; I am no better than my ancestors.' Then he lay down under the tree and fell asleep. (1 Kings 19:3–5 NIV)

A conversation with a youth worker in a nearby statutory project was a sobering experience. He was quitting. Having worked with young people for many years he was finally at his wit's end. During the youth club he had asked a young person to leave the building and afterwards this individual had made a death threat against him, which he was taking seriously. He had had enough.

Whilst this is perhaps an extreme incident, many workers come under intense pressure when working with young people who consistently manifest challenging behaviour. The ongoing nature of some of these issues and the worker's response to them can lead to a downward spiral, which might look something like the following:

> Stressful event leads to ⟶ negative thoughts, feelings and reactions
> which lead to ⟶ inappropriate responses
> which produce ⟶ further stressful events

By way of illustration, let us imagine a young person letting off a fire extinguisher. This would inevitably cause disturbance, mayhem and stress. In an ideal world, the worker would remain calm, clear the area, negotiate with the young person and organize the clearing up of the mess. However, a worker 'on the edge' is far more likely to shout at the young person and engage in an argument with them about their behaviour. Other young people might then join in and some might start laughing at what has happened (if they were not laughing already!). This could further inflame the worker, who might then focus anger on some of the other young people, creating a barrier and increasing the tension and stress of the event.

Even workers experiencing significant success within a project can be worn down by the demands of ongoing challenging behaviour. In the Scripture quoted above, Elijah's desperate plea follows a glorious victory over the prophets of Baal. Elijah has just witnessed God at work in significant ways, yet a threat from the manipulative and evil queen Jezebel sends him spiralling emotionally down. If youth work is to be sustainable and workers are to survive for the long haul, they will need to give consideration to developing the necessary strategies and skills for reducing and managing their own stress. The following can be helpful here.

- There is no substitute for robust self-awareness. Understanding their own responses to stress, and identifying any particular triggers (those things guaranteed to wind them up) will help youth workers manage their own emotional responses in conflict situations. Similarly understanding their normal response to anger—internalizing, exploding, suppressing—will enable them to both respond at the time in a measured way and/or ensure that unexpressed issues are worked through at a later date.
- Learning to separate the young people from the problems is vital, particularly in situations where there feels to be any kind of 'personal' attack involved.
- Having appropriate support in place should provide a context in which issues can be discussed and explored in a less stressful environment. This may include formal supervision, good friends and other youth workers who may be able to act in a 'sounding board' role.
- Workers need to look after themselves physically, particularly when faced with stressful situations. Inadequate sleep, food, drink, rest or exercise will simply increase stress. Interestingly, if we read on in Elijah's situation, we find God attending first of all to Elijah's physical needs, before speaking specifically to him about strategies for addressing the problem at hand. Similarly, finding effective ways of switching off, relaxing and unwinding will not necessarily solve the problem, but will help to put things into perspective.
- Team meetings to de-brief, set goals and discuss strategies are very important as part of a long-term approach to challenging behaviour issues. This might include post-session de-briefs and longer strategic planning opportunities. It may also be helpful to access further training in areas which are a particular challenge.
- Maintaining a sense of perspective is also a key factor in reducing stress. Revisiting God's call to the work, remembering the motivating factors—prayer, reflection and nurturing spirituality.

Conclusions

8

Mission in the UK no longer finds the Christian message and viewpoint the dominant narrative and we must bear this in mind when working with young people.

The days of a cosy cost-free approach to reaching people are gone and dealing with challenging behaviours might be one of the prices we have to pay. Drawing a parallel with some missions movements of the past may be helpful. Life expectancy in Africa in the 18th and 19th centuries was short as missionaries ventured into unknown places visiting unknown tribes. Many were killed, struck by disease, forgotten and some were even eaten! If the most we have to put up with is the odd broken window, or bit of verbal abuse, then, in a historical sense, we have got off lightly.

Workers need to model the standards expected in a Christ-like manner. Equally, churches and organizations need to take their responsibilities seriously and seek to create an environment in which the work, the workers and the young people themselves can flourish. In many ways, the problems will not disappear if and when the young people come to faith. The book of Acts illustrates very clearly some of the interesting dynamics faced by a growing church flourishing in a culture previously untouched by the gospel. Processes of discipleship and spiritual growth are likely to be equally challenging, but also exciting and rewarding for all those involved.

Churches, organizations, projects, leaders and workers must carefully weigh up the cost of working with this cohort of young people. It is not an easy ride and it is very demanding. The results can be life changing, inspiring and motivating, but there might well be a few bumpy journeys on the road before the destination is reached. Jesus always reached out to those who were struggling. Many had behavioural issues—including the disciples closest to him. He never shirked away from tough decisions, challenges and confrontations but equally never gave up on being compassionate. He was infinitely patient with those in need and only seems to have lost his temper with the religious people of the day. Maybe we can learn from this as we seek to engage with and make a difference to those young people we work with who exhibit challenging behaviour.

Further Useful Resources

S Adirondack, *Just About Managing* (London: London Voluntary Service Council, 1998)

Churches Child Protection Advisory Service (www.ccpas.co.uk)

D Goleman, *Emotional Intelligence* (London: Bloomsbury Publishing Plc, 1996)

G Finch, *Top Tips: Managing Difficult Behaviour* (Bletchley: Scripture Union, 2005)

G Ingram and J Harris, *Delivering Good Youth Work* (Lyme Regis: Russell House Publishing, 2001)

K Keenan, *The Management Guide to Understanding Behaviour* (Horsham: Ravette Publishing Limited, 1996)

F Macbeth and N Fine, *Playing with Fire: Creative Conflict Resolution for Young Adults* (Gabriola Island: New Society Publishers, 1995)

N Thompson, *People Skills* (London: Macmillan Press Ltd, 1996)

Training Manual in Community Mediation Skills (Mediation UK, 1995)

Websites: www.adhdmatters.co.uk
           www.homeoffice.gov.uk/justice/victims/restorative/
           www.restorativejustice.org
           www.restorativejustice.org.uk
           www.youngminds.org.uk/adhd

Notes

1   R Passmore, *Meet Them Where They're At* (Bletchley: Scripture Union, 2003) p 38

2   *Young People Now*, 13–19 October 2004, pp 16–17

3   The same article suggests that only 26% of young people admit to committing a crime and of those only 7% involved the police and only a minority were violent.

4   See for example *A failure of justice: reducing child imprisonment* (2003), *Counting the cost: reducing child imprisonment* (2003) and *A better alternative: reducing child imprisonment* (2005) all published by Nacro, www.nacro.org.uk

5   *Anti-Social Behaviour* (Youth Justice Board, 2005) p 10

6   D J Bosch (New York: Orbis Books, 1991) *Transforming Mission* p 10

7   Further information on restorative justice can be found in the web sites listed in the resources section above. See www.restorativejustice.org www.restorativejustice.org.uk and www.homeoffice.gov.uk/justice/victims/restorative/

8   CCPAS Advice—Working with Disruptive Children.